# "Live Like a Monk Outside the Walls"

By
**Father Karl Pruter**

**BORGO PRESS / WILDSIDE PRESS**

www.wildsidepress.com

# Table of Contents

# Who is a Monk?

A monk is someone who has dedicated his life to worship and service of God for his own sake

That seems simple enough. To be a monk you don't have to go to any special place, you need not belong to a particular order, or even to a particular church. Of course, you follow Christ, belong to his body and the Holy Church, and dedicate your life to worship and to the service of God.

In this respect you are not any different from any other follower of Christ. What sets you apart is that what God expects of you. You do not become a monk to flee the world, to pray for salvation of others and the world, or even to save your own soul. You do it, because you believed that this is the why of your creation. God created us to love Him, to worship Him, and to serve him. There is no other purpose for our being.

We do, of course, serve others because we love God. By the same token we pray for the state of the whole world, because it is God's world and as He cares for it, so must we. A monk's life revolves around God and in everything he says and does, he seeks direction from God.

A monk's prayers are prayers of adoration. Pure adoration seeks no reward. Although, from time to time, we may petition God to protect us from harm, heal our infirmities or help us in our need. There are many contemplative orders of monks and nuns, although since Vatican II their numbers have declined alarmingly. Many critics have said it is selfish and wrong to shut oneself behind the walls of a cloister in order to find salvation through prayer and contemplation. Many of the contemplative orders have attempted to justify their way of life by pointing out that they spend many hours praying for others, both the living and the dead.

But the monk does not need any justification. We are all called by God to pray. Indeed, we are told to pray without ceasing. It is fallacious to believe that the monk or nun who lives in a cloister is abandoning the world. First, by their prayers they contribute to everyone's salvation, but secondly, and equally important by choosing to live a disciplined life either within or without the walls the monk or nun gives a silent, but effective witness to God. They are saying, "Nothing is as important as praying and serving God." The monastery stands as a silent, and mysterious witness, to those who busily and hastily pass by but who may never find even a few minutes for prayer.

Many monks and nuns outside the walls devote their lives, even as they pray to feeding and clothing the poor. They know, what many have forgotten, that to give a man bread that is unblessed by prayer, is to give a stale crust indeed. One of the reasons why the monk values work so highly is that it enables him to contribute to the feeding of the hungry and clothing the poor. Work has a peculiar place in the monk's life. His first reason for working is that he may earn his daily bread. He, like all men, takes from the earth for sustenance, but he feels deeply that he must give something back. Even more, not only must his labor provide for himself but he does additional labor that he might be able to help the man who cannot labor or whose labors is compensated so poorly that he cannot adequately provide for himself or his family.

Labor makes one more like God, for God did labor to create the universe and he labors so that that it may continue and that all his creatures may be provided for. Nothing exists unless God labored to create it. Nothing is conceived, or grows, or reproduces unless God wills it. If the seed sprouts it is the work of God. He expects us to till the soil, plant the seed, weed, and water until the harvest. It is truly one of the wonderful partnerships between God and man. The creator expects to care and to groom the earth which he gave us. There are those who worship the earth and call it, " mother " but the monk worships the creator of the earth, and calls him, father.

To the monk prayer and work are one. He communicates with God by words and by the work of his hands. For his labor is a gift to God and although silent it speaks to God of his love for him. Many critics over the centuries have said that, the monks and the nuns who are cloistered, give too much time to prayer. They do not understand that these folk are immersed in prayer, and it is true that their prayers are said while they are engaged in work. Do not say that both cannot be done at once. For if a man can play a guitar and sing, surely he can do many other things and silently or audibly sing his praises to God.

The monk does not deify work. He knows it is not an end in itself. If his work does not glorify God, he will not do it. So many laborers dislike what they are doing because they are doing it for someone they do not like and respect, or simply to earn a paycheck. The monk's approach to work is quite serious.

First he must be certain that he has received his vocation from God. Secondly, all that he does must give glory to God, and finally he must use the fruits of his labor as God directs.

It does not matter if he is an entrepreneur. His undertaking is for God. Therefore he will not be greedy, but will try to generate enough profit to meet his needs and to be able too give to the needy and to the causes which God may direct him to support. He knows that he actually owns nothing. What material goods or money is in his possession are not his. They belong to God and the monk is merely the steward. He must exercise his stewardship carefully. He cannot engage in just any trade but only in those trades which God approves. Nor can he invest his money in any industry or business, except God approves. To invest in the manufacture of military equipment, or chemicals so dangerous they cannot be sold in his own country but he is allowed to ship them abroad, would be contrary to a life committed to Christ.

He respects the earth and if he is a farmer he is anxious to preserve the land which provides him with a bountiful harvest. He spurns chemicals which pollute the streams and lakes and, where necessary, practices crop rotation. In return the land is good to him.

The line is not always easily discerned. He may be a bartender, but he must exercise care and not to permit his costumers to drink to excess. In some states this obligation is written into law, but for the monk it is written on his heart as well. Other more harmful drugs are forbidden to him. He cannot use them, make them or sell them. Currently we rail against big

4

tobacco and we should. But should the grocer who sells tobacco also be held responsible?

For the monk work is never just a job. For him there is something sacred about the tasks which God has given him perform. First, he regards it as vital, necessary and useful, for God does not hand out jobs just to keep us busy there is a reason behind every assignment given to us by God. The monk therefore will make certain that it is well done. And by his labor he will witness to the world. Who will not wonder at seeing a laborer who is serious about his every task and shows joy and enthusiasm for even the most menial task. But why shouldn't he? Kahlil Gibran has said " If you cannot work with love but only with distaste, it is better that you should leave your work and sit at the gate of the temple and take alms of those who work with joy."[1] The monk is not so concerned about what he does, but for whom he does it. By the same token he is not working for a paycheck but since the money is God's he remembers that God's Son said, " A laborer is worthy of his hire."

The monk in his work mixes the sacred and the secular while doing a menial task. Others observing him frequently remark how carefully he performs his job and how serene and joyous he seems in doing his work. Frequently they are drawn to him and ask him about his life and may even ask how he manages to maintain such an even and joyous disposition. This affords the monk an opportunity to witness concerning his commitment to and his faith in God.

---

[1] "The Prophet", Kahlil Gibran, Alfred A. Knopf, New York, 1941 page 30.

One Monk felt called to engage in missionary work throughout the area in which he lives. Unfortunately neither he nor the church he serves had funds for the travel that would be involved. After much prayer he sought a sales position that would necessitate travel throughout the area. When he is obligated by his secular job to visit a new community he goes and does his work and then spends time to acquaint himself with the community and seek out any who might be searching for God. He notes the number of closed churches and seeks to learn about them. (i.e. why they closed and about people who might be left without a church home because of the church's closing.)

But above all he prays for those without faith. He prays for the last of he least, of the lost. It may take a while before, he will meet them, but, his prayers shall be answered. At this stage of his mission he has met a number of people who are searching for God, for faith and for church they can call their own. He prays that soon they shall find all three.

Then monk is called to be many things. As we said in the beginning he is simply some one who has dedicated his life to worship and to the services of God for its own sake. For him God is sufficient.

So first of all, the monk prays. It is through prayer that we live with God. It is through prayer that we have fellowship with God. It is through prayer that God is able to move our hearts and out minds. Unless we pray we cannot have a sense of direction. We, and the entire universe revolve around God. And when we, or any part of the universe does not, we become disconnected from the one who gives stability to all and to everything.

The monk also works, he worships and he loves his own. Family and community mean much to him. He, unlike many, in out society loves even his enemies. It would seem that the monk is very much involved in the world and he is. But he is also separated from family, friends, and the world because for him is God is sufficient. In following Christ, he has chosen him to be first in his life. He has heeded the command to leave father, mother, brother, and sister in order that he may love and serve the God who gave him life and who first loved him. Whether behind walls or outside the walls, God is everything to the monk. Nothing else matters, yet everything matters because of his love for God. A monk sees the whole world through the eyes of God.

# The Monk Works

" Work, for the night is coming. Work, thro' the morning hours. Work ' mid apringing flowers. Work when the day grows brighter, work in the flowing sun; Work, for the night is coming, When man's work is done."

It was difficult to decide whether the monk's work should be included in the chapter on prayer or whether to include it in this book as a separate chapter. For to the monk, prayer and work are one. All prayer is prayer of the lips, the heart, the mind, and the hands. Normally, in prayers the hands are folded reverently, but in work which is also a form of prayer the hands play a more active role.

The monk believes he has been not only called to work, but also that he is called to a particular vocation. God has created every man for a purpose. For the monk, the question of for whom shall I work has already been answered. He works for God; and it is God whom he first must please. And because of this he takes seriously his stewardship toward the customers or public whom he also serves. But before beginning his work, he offers a simple prayer for direction. The following is typical, but perhaps, you have one of your own.

"Lord, Heavenly Father, guide me in my work today, that what I produce may be pleasing to Thee. May my work be also done efficiently so that people may afford my work and that my employer may earn a fair profit ; and that I, your servant, may earn  fair wage.

Amen,"

During the day, the monk will keep his heart and mind on God. From time to time when he can, he will silently offer ejaculations such as:

"Lord, have mercy on me a sinner!" Christ, have mercy on me a sinner! Lord, may my work be a witness for Thee."

The monk will not only do his labor well, but he will do it cheerfully. If he cannot find joy in his work, he should give thought and prayer so that he may know if he has chosen the right vocation. If he is in the cannot find joy in his work, he should give thought and prayer so that he may know if he has chosen the right vocation. If he has not he must seek to discover what his God –given vocation is. If he is in the right vocation, he must pray that God would show him the joy in what he is doing. Many years ago, a railroad porter hated his job because he through it was demeaning. After some prayers he realized that God was him this work to do so that, through his service to people, he could witness to them concerning Jesus Christ and the call to His Heavenly Kingdom. Here was a true apostle of Christ. Unlike other Princes of the Church, he was not given a Cardinal's red hat; but ironically, porters in those days were called "Red Caps" which was the color of the caps they wore. And for this humble evangelist for Christ, it was sufficient.

A number of years ago, a man wrote to me that he felt called to become a priest so that he might minister to the lost sheep in his area. When I asked him how many he had won for Christ, he replied, " As a mere layman I can do nothing.

Furthermore to start a parish property, I need to be incorporated; and that I can't afford to do." Neither statement was true. Christ can use us all in whatever position in life we may be. In fact, most non-believers who are won to Christ are won through the efforts of dedicated lay men and women. All of us listen more intently to the Gospel when the words are spoken by a lay member of the church.

As a pastor, I used to call on every new person who moved to the community and invited them to come to church. Often I was successful, but if a lay member gave an invitation, "Would you like to attend church with me some Sunday?", he was twice as likely to succeed.

The monk outside of the walls is God's most formidable evangelist. Paul the tent maker was far more successful among the Gentiles then either Peter or John Mark. His simple occupation of tent maker may have had something to so with it; because in the secular world it was regarded as "useful" and unfortunately, priests are seldom given that accolade.

It is fortunate that the monk knows which activities are most important. Others may admire his secular work, but he knows that his prayers are far more precious. In the show " Mash", Father Mulcahy was asked to help in the operating room. After the experience he was on cloud nine, because he viewed his lending his two hands as far greater help than his offering of the sacraments or his many prayers. This was TV's negative witness. People in trouble often need another pair of hands, and for this they don't need monks. It is for troubles far greater, which only for God can heal, they seek holy men and women to pray for them, to bring the sacraments, or just to be close to someone who reflects the peace and serenity of one who lives close to God. The monks true witness is not in the words he speaks, but in the life he lives. Prayer and work are his most important activities; but there are also others that fill his days and his life.

# The Monk Prays

The monk is a man of prayer. He lives for God and his life must be with God. How can anyone be with God and not continually converse with him? For a God to whom we do not speak, and who does not speak to us, is not God at all, but a false image.

In our times there was a movement that said, "God is dead". It was at first glance a stupid thing to say, but God who is ignored, a god to whom we do not pray and who in no manner affects out lives is truly not the living God of the Bible, not the God who created heaven and earth, and not the God who Jesus call, "Father."

We are blessed, if we believe in God, and we need to take advantage of that blessing. For the creator of heaven and earth does not ignored the works of his creation. He is truly a God of Love and he bids us to come to him in love and in prayer.

The Prayers of the monk are simple. He begins each day by acknowledging that God has brought us safely to the beginning of the day and he seeks God's direction and protection in the day ahead. It is not how he says it that is important for all prayers of a true monk are kept simple. They may be extemporaneous or may read the age-old prayers which say succinctly the thoughts which he wishes to convey to God. A typical monk's prayer at the beginning of each day is as follows.

"O Lord, our Heavenly Father, Almighty and Everlasting God, who hast safely brought us to the beginning of this day, defend us in the same with thy mighty power and grant that this day we fall into no sin, neither run into any kind of danger, but that all our doings, being ordered by thy governance may be righteous in thy sight; through Jesus Christ, our Lord. Amen."

How better could we begin our day with God? The monk reads such prayer as this because it says perfectly what he wants to say to God at the beginning of the day. He could extemporize but he chooses not to because he realizes that, " A perfect prayer brings forth a perfect answer, and an imperfect prayer brings forth an imperfect answer."

Now depending on what God expects of him in the day which he is beginning the monk, if time permits will offer others prayers. It must be remembered that the monk also gives service to God by his labor. That too, is a time of prayer and we shall discuss this later. But for now let me offer you some prayers which a monk offer at the day's beginning

A Prayer of Adoration

"Suffer not my heart, O Lord, which was made only for Thee, which is entirely the work of thy hands, to belong to any other but Thee, or to love anything equally or in preference to Thee, Thy delight is to be with the children of men, and why is not thy presence my felicity? Why art Thou not more to me than all things else—Thou: who art my only and sovereign good? I am resolved henceforth absolutely to love Thee alone. I will be all Thine, seek to please Thee in all things, and breathe only Thy love. Amen?"

Thomas A' Kempis

A Prayer of St. Francis

"O Lord, out Christ, may we have thy mind and thy spirit; make us instruments of thy peace; where there is hatred let us sow love; where there is injury, pardon; where there is discord, union, where there is doubt, faith, where there is despair, hope where there is darkness, light, and where there is sadness, joy.

O Divine Master, grant that we may not so much seek to be consoled as to console; to be understood as to understand; to be loved, as to love; for it in pardoning that we are pardoned; and it is dying that we were born to eternal life. Amen"

The monk's prayers will very, for each day has its own needs and challenges. The monk, foe example, may know of a friend's or acquaintance's problem. He would therefore offer a prayer such as follows:

"Lord, Heavenly Father give to Thy servant ......, the desire to draw closer to Thee, so that he may receive the inspiration of Thu holy Spirit, and so solve his present problem according to Thy light and Direction. Amen."

Note that the prayer does not merely ask that his friend resolve his problem but that his friend resolve his problem but that he do so according to God's Light and Direction. This is what is meant by " A perfect prayer brings forth a perfect answer."

The monk prays for his local parish for he knows that Christ commanded him to preach the gospel to all men. It is through his parish church that he can best achieve this aim.

## A Prayer For The Parish Church

"Lord, Heavenly Father, we are ever mindful of thy commanded that we go forth and preach the Gospel to all men. Grant us, who have been directed by thy Holy Spirit to serve thee as members of_____(parish) thy continual guidance that this church may be the instrument for the redemption of many. May those who live in the community respond to Christ's invitation to come to His Holy Table, as well as the stranger who while passing through our community may stop and visit Thy House. In Jesus Name, we pray. Amen.

+++

# The Monk Sings

They haven't done a movie yet entitled, "The Singing Monk", but our world has rediscovered the wonderful chants and the songs of the monk. Just as the church has reached its lowest ebb in centuries, the ancient chants of the monks are being heard and sung. This time, not in isolated monasteries but on tapes and CD's in homes around the world.

The monk sings for his enjoyment but more importantly because it is a part of his calling and his life. Because his life is determined by God and by God's Scriptures he sings praise to God. He heeds the admonition in Psalm 149 to, "Praise yea the Lord. Sing unto the Lord a new song, and his praise in the congregation of the saints." And again in Psalm 81:1-3 " Sing aloud unto God our strength; make joyful noise unto God of Jacob. Take a psalm, and bring hither the timbrel, the pleasant harp with the psaltery. Blow up the trumpet in the new moon, in the time appointed on our solemn feast day."

And again, from I Samuel 16:23

" And it came to pass, when the evil spirit was upon Saul, that Davis took a harp and played with his hand; so Saul was refreshed and was well, and the evil departed from him."

The three texts above call attention to the two uses of music which are mentioned in Holy Scripture. First, it is a fitting way to praise God, and secondly, it can bring to us healing and refreshment. About fifty years ago when I worked as a recreational therapist in mental institution they were talking

17

about the musical therapy. Someone had re-discovered what David and Saul knew centuries ago, that music can heal troubled minds.

Oddly enough many sectarian churches banned musical instrument from public worship. Among them the churches of Christ, and some Presbyterian denominations. They tell the story of a man who belonged to a small church in Vermont that by tradition never had a musical instrument but finally decided to install an organ. The man was incensed and left the church bitterly denouncing the church board and the pastor. He felt, however that he should give honor and glory to God on Sunday and he elected to attend the local Methodist Church. He began to attend there regularly much to the bewilderment of the Methodist minister. Finally the minister called on him and stated that he was pleased that he was attending church so faithfully, but he could not understand. He said, " Sandy, I understand you left the Presbyterian Church because they installed an organ. But we have had one in our church for many years, and we play it at every service and, yet, you have chosen to worship with us. I am pleased, but I don't understand."

"Well pastor, " Sandy replied, "It is very simple. " I think it is all right to have an organ in the Methodist meeting house, but no organ should be played in the House of the Lord."

It is sad that Sandy didn't know either his scriptures well, nor the history of the church. Obviously musical instruments were part of the worship in the temple and then surely so in the early church. In his life, Jesus encountered musical instruments in the Temple and in secular life. He attended weddings and other functions where music was an integral part. The early church and down through the Churches history, not only, had musical instruments, but also was a patron of many arts and gave lavishly to musicians and composers. Much of the great music was composed as settings for the mass and for other offices of the church. And the monks were among those who played and composed music for the glory of God.

The Church and the philosophers in the Medieval times and the Renaissance saw music as the monks do, not only as an aid to worship, but also as reflection of his life force and as a means of expressing the harmony between God and man. Thus, by definition, good music is capable of turning man's mind and heart toward God. It would follow then that bad music would appeal to man's baser nature and actually turn his thoughts away from God. From philosophical view music is not just a matter of taste but all music that is harmonious with the Divine is good and any music that disturbs that harmony is simply bad music. One cannot put spiritual verses spiritual verses to bad music and except to bring men and women closer to God. It takes the right words put to the right music to be uplifting.

All of us can recall moments when we heard a truly great orchestra, or a singer who literally lifted our minds and hearts heavenward. It has been said that "Music hath charms to soothe the savage beast." And it is so, but put in the words of the unknown written in 1910, "Music uplifts the mind to higher things. With many a grown man and women, one of the fondest recollections is the memory of many happy evenings at home, given to the enjoyment of music of various character." Unfortunately musical evenings at home have almost disappeared since the advent of television. It was a bad trade; and we are all poorer because of it.

It has been said that if one could control the music that is played and heard in any nation, he could influence that nation for good or for evil. Today, we commonly say that what we are is determined by what we eat, or what we read, and each in its own way is true. But, music may be a more powerful influence than either. Certainly the Church should consider it in planning its program of evangelism. Some time, I would like to see our Church sponsor a radio or TV program built almost entirely around the great music of the Church. A program build around the great church music of Palestrina would prove far more effective in winning people to God, than many sermons. Sermons come form the tongues of men; music speaks with the tongues of angels. It can as the philosophers have said, "Bring us in harmony with God."

So the monk sings and whether alone or in chorus he seeks to be in rhythm and in harmony with God. Alone in the forest or in the meadow when he sings he knows he is not alone but he is singing and walking with his Lord.

## The Monk Contemplates and Meditates

St. Francis de Sales dedicated his wonderful book on prayer, "To the Most Holy Trinity Who Created All Things for the Sake of Prayer". Of course, we know that of all God's creatures only man seeks to communicate with Him. Only man seems capable of prayer, contemplation and meditation. But when we examine these three functions, de Sales' statement becomes clear because prayer comes not only from our hearts and minds, but comes from every experience we have in the world in which God chose to place us. The sum total of what a man is, and does and experiences goes into every prayer which he utters.

In a sermon, entitled "The Goal of Prayer" he says, "We say simply that (prayer) is so useful and necessary that without it we would not come to any good, seeing that by means of prayer we are shown how to perform all our actions well."[2] In short it is not possible for us to know the will of God for us unless we pray. Elsewhere He has given us general rules by which we must live but He knows we cannot do it alone, but there is the ever present need to know what He wills for each man and each woman. Sainthood is not achieved by any man unless he walks hand in hand with his Creator and for the monk there is no other reason to exist.

The Monk is truly a man of prayer and as Christ directed his prayers are unceasing. They not only take place in the observe of the services of Prime, Matins, Vespers and Compline but usually after each of these, if he has the opportunity to

---

[2] Fiorelli, Lewis S., editor, "The Sermons of St. Francis de Sales on Prayer", Tan Books, Rockford 1985, page 1.

observe them he will have more personal prayers and devotions. His prayers are often followed by contemplation and meditation. Now what is meant by these two very important words? As we learn more and more about God and experience His many blessings we are drawn to contemplate the wonder of God and His blessings upon us. The Christian cannot help but recall the life of Jesus Christ, as revealed by Holy Scripture, his heart and mind are moved to imitate the life which Christ has revealed to us.

The monk cannot help but move to the next step which is meditation. "What", he asks, "Does this mean? And how can I follow in His footsteps?" What the monk seeks more than anything else is to be with God, the Father, even as Christ is with the Father. Then, and then only, will he know what God wills for him.

To believe in God means nothing to the monk, unless he can also do the will of God. By this, he means, not only in the large decisions of life, but in every little detail of his daily life.

One of the characteristics of a good monk is the manner in which he uses his time. He tries to be a good steward of tall his resources. He knows it is important to manage what little money he has and equally important to manage time, perhaps everyone's most valuable possession. Whereas, others complain they do not have sufficient time to pray frequently, the monk so controls his time, that he has time for unceasing prayers. For example, he uses what I call "fret time." Notice people in a physician's or a dentist's waiting room. They sit and fret and they may even fume and complain. Waiting they see as wasted time, and for them it is. They either read an out-dated magazine which may not interest them or spend the time starring in space and watching the clock.

For the monk this time is welcomed for now he can contemplate God and His blessings and meditate in order to be close to God and to discover His Will for His humble monk. It is ironic that this time, is for the monk a glorious time spent in the presence of God. What man or woman would see any time spent with someone they loved as wasted time. Likewise one who loves God is thrilled on every occasion when he can find a moment to spend in God's presence. Think of all the times there are in the day to do what the monk does. In the car going to and from work. Maybe, in a traffic jam, or waiting at a stop light. Unable to do our appointed task because of a delay in delivery or because some sub-contractor is behind in his work. One man, who is perhaps a monk outside the walls without knowing it, stopped by the Cathedral of the Prince of Peace and asked if there was something he could do to be of help. He had come from out of state to work on a project but was unable to for a few days until a sub-contractor finished his task. He wanted to use the waiting time to serve God. As he was a stone mason, I told him I needed help in our Garden of Saints in building a wall around the statue of Our Lady of Guadalupe. Together we spent two days and the wall is a beautiful addition to the Garden where hundreds of people visit annually. For both of us it was a time when we could pray with our hands as we gave God an offering of our labor.

The monk wastes no hours. He never kills time, although, time not spent with God, he may begrudge. The least valuable hours which he spends are probably those which he does almost solely for pay. The paid employment is valued most, when it makes a contribution to society, as well as bringing a fair return. The farmer or the monk in tilling the soil rejoices, first, because he is doing what God has called him to do and then because he is feeding his family, and a countless multitude.

There are many "monks" outside the walls. They may be farmers, masons, mechanics, factory workers, clerks, and, maybe, a tent maker or two. But all have in common, the Christian conviction, that God is at the center of their lives. There is no wall to shut out the world, but they are not part of the world, because of their nearness to God, he has become the only world to which they give unquestioned allegiance, and obedience. In so doing they reject the pleasures of this world, so that they may experience joy that comes from the practice of the presence of God. They have traded finite pleasures for the infinite and eternal joy with the Almighty and Everlasting God.

# The Monk's Library

THE IMITATION OF CHRIST
By Thomas A'Kempis

NEW SEEDS OF CONTEMPLATION
By Thomas Merton

SPIRITUAL MAXIMS
By Nicholas Grou

THEOLOGIA GERMANICA
Anonymous 14 century writer

THE CLOUD OF UNKNOWING
Anonymous 14 century writer

PENSEES
By Blaise Pascal

DARK NIGHT OF THE SOUL
By St. John of the Cross

THE MYSTICAL PATH
By Karl Pruter

THE PRACTICE OF THE PRESENCE OF GOD
By Brother Lawrence

THE PROPHET
By Kahlil Gibran

HOLY WISDOM
By Austine Baker

THE CONFESSIONS
By Jacob Boehme

THE JERUSALEM COMMUNITY RULE OF LIFE
By Pierre-Marie Delfeux

# A Monk is Frugal

A monk who lives outside the walls knows all the hardships and frustrations of living in the world. His first vocation, always, is his service to God. His mind is at rest knowing who he is and whom he serves. His second vocation is not always so easily discerned. It must, of course, be honest, provide sufficient income for himself and his family, and never be so demanding that he must neglect his obligations to God and to his family.

What pay he receives he perceives as coming as a loan from God. And therefore he must be frugal. One does not squander resources belonging to another. The monk recognizes that all he has is not his, but belongs to God and therefore he is required to be a good steward.

His stewardship is not only for the resources placed into his hands; but also for those in the environment. He saves on electricity, for example, in order to reduce his electric bill, but also to save the world's resources. In most cases, coal is spent to produce the electric power. Its use may never affect him; but its waste may affect future generations.

It is amazing how wasteful we have become. Yes, the monk may live in the world, but not live like most. He is extremely frugal. He is never stingy; but it is because of his frugal living that he has the means to give alms.

When the monk arises in the morning, he has a frugal, although adequate, breakfast. When needed he turns the heat on to 68 degrees. He has chosen an adequate but inexpensive heating system. If he lives in a rural area where wood is cheap, he will heat as much of the house as he can with wood. If he needs other heating he chooses natural gas, if available, propane if not. Electricity, almost anywhere, he feels is both beyond his means and extravagant when used for heating.

The monk is a careful shopper. He is aware of the price of everything; and he goes where he can get the best price. He is in the lines at Aldi's; and he buys in quantity so he will not have to make too many trips to the store. He keeps his eyes open for sale items and buys the house brand when it is competitively priced. He buys fruits and vegetables in season. If he has land where he can grow vegetables and he has sufficient time; he will cultivate a garden. But the monk will always consider his priorities, and would not have a garden if it took him away from other prime activities. His time is God's time; and God chooses how, when and where he shall serve Him.

In buying clothing he is careful to buy practical garments that have lasting quality. Many years ago I was in need of a new black suit. I looked in the stores and was shocked by the prices. It had been many years since I had felt the need of a new suit, and inflation had taken its toll. Finally, I called a man who was the best dressed man in the area. I felt he might be able to help me find a place where, even if the prices were not cheap, at least I would get my money's worth. When I told him my reason, my situation, and explained why I was calling him, he was much amused. He told me that he bought nearly all his suits and coats in the used clothing stores.

If the monk moves often, he needs to become acquainted with the local stores. The best way, usually, is to ask a native who seems frugal; and he will normally be happy to share with you his knowledge of the local stores.

The monk is always aware of his responsibility as a steward. Therefore, he keeps accounts. Many people who have financial troubles do not keep any kind of record of their expenditures. I have heard them justify not doing so because they say they have so little to spend that it is not necessary. But it is even more so if your income is small. They do not keep accounts because they do not wish to face their situation, consequently, they compound their problems in many ways. They frequently have overdrafts because they "forgot" to enter a check in the check register. They lose track of what they spend; and long before the next pay check, their money is gone. The monk tries to be responsible and even if it goes against the grain he keeps careful accounts. "What is the purpose," you say, "in knowing where the money went if it is gone?" well, first, it shows us those areas where we are spending far more than we can afford; and we can avoid doing so with the next pay check. It also reveals where we are spending money for luxuries which we cannot afford. I have a friend who has a very meager income that is far below the poverty line. Yet he spends money on luxuries which, I know, I cannot afford. For example, call waiting and cable television. I have never mentioned either of these two items and referred to them as extravagant. Of course, I realize that different people spend their money in different ways. But it is these different ways that are the root of our financial problems. We all need to spend money as God directs. For each, His direction will differ; but His direction will never lead us into extravagant spending and living beyond our means. If God helps you prepare your budget I can assure you that you will not bounce checks and the pay, however meager, will last until the end of the month. The monk has to let God into every aspect of his life; and since God chooses his work and directs his spending, he seldom has a financial crisis for which he needs to pray to God for help in solving it. His life of prayer, and that includes every aspect of living, prevents the many crisis, which cause so many to turn to God in panic. Thus the monk leads a calm and peaceful existence.

From time to time many monks feel that they are burdened by the need to earn their daily bread. They have had a considerable amount of success in leading people to Christ. As Andrew brought Peter to Jesus, they have been on the front line of evangelism and introduced many to Christ. They begin to think that, if only they did not have to hold a secular job, they could do so much more. The world is filled with hungry people needing to know Christ. If the monk feels he is called to serve as a full time evangelist, then he must prepare himself to enter the priesthood where he would evangelize and serve those he has brought to Christ. But he must be certain of his call. For as a monk, he gives witness not only by words and example, but also by his work and his frugality. Let him be certain of one thing. He lives by faith, knowing that God will enable him to earn enough for his daily needs and enough to be able to give service and witness to others.

Let me clarify the phrase "Live by faith." There are times when some few are called to a ministry for which they see no immediate support, but feel asked by God to undertake a venture in faith. It may be to start up a soup kitchen, a hostel for the homeless or some other social service. They may say, and correctly so, that "As God guides, God provides." When it is God who guides, they are never disappointed. That, of course, is the first caveat: If it truly is God who is guiding our monk, he dare not refuse.

But before taking such a venture in faith, he needs to share his vision with other monks and ask for their prayers and their critique of his vision. He needs also to ask whether he is moving ahead on his faith or relying solely of the faith of others. If the first, he is serving God; but if the second, he has become a beggar seeking only to live a life style that he has chosen, rather than one God has chosen for him.

One other comment. I do not believe there can be people who are exclusively evangelists. I believe, if we call people to Christ, we have a responsibility to be their shepherd or to find one for them. The latter is not always possible. If the monk feels he is called to do nothing else but evangelize, he needs to prepare himself to be a pastor so he can meet the needs of those he brought to Christ and be able to feed them, that is, to administer the sacraments and to meet their daily and occasional spiritual needs.

He needs to know that as a lay monk, earning his daily bread, he is often more effective than any pastor who is supported by the Church. A monk who works in a factory or an office is seen as someone who knows how hard it is to work in the market place. In the eyes of many his witness has more credibility than those laborers in the vineyard who are seen as hirelings. When a priest speaks about God, it is expected of him.  But when a monk, outside the walls, speaks of God lay people see him as one of their own and they listen with greater interest.

Some monks will be called to be full time pastors; but whether as a full time pastor or one who holds a secular job, the monk works and serves his fellow man--- In the Name of God. +kp

www.ingramcontent.com/pod-product-compliance
Lightning Source LLC
LaVergne TN
LVHW091211080426
835509LV00006B/938